WHAT ARE FOOD CHAINS & FOOD WEBS?

LOUISE SPILSBURY

Britannica
Educational Publishing

IN ASSOCIATION WITH

ROSEN
EDUCATIONAL SERVICES

Published in 2014 by Britannica Educational Publishing (a trademark of Encyclopædia Britannica, Inc.) in association with The Rosen Publishing Group, Inc.
29 East 21st Street, New York, NY 10010

Distributed exclusively by Rosen Publishing.
To see additional Britannica Educational Publishing titles, go to rosenpublishing.com

First Edition

Britannica Educational Publishing
J.E. Luebering: Director, Core Reference Group
Anthony L. Green: Editor, Compton's by Britannica

Rosen Publishing
Hope Lourie Killcoyne: Executive Editor
Nelson Sá: Art Director

Library of Congress Cataloging-in-Publication Data

Spilsbury, Louise, author.
What are food chains & food webs? / Louise Spilsbury. — First edition.
    pages cm. — (Let's find out. Life science)
Audience: Grades 3 to 6.
Includes bibliographical references and index.
ISBN 978-1-62275-236-2 (library binding) — ISBN 978-1-62275-239-3 (pbk.) — ISBN 978-1-62275-240-9 (6-pack)
1. Food chains (Ecology)—Juvenile literature. I. Title. II. Title: What are food chains and food webs.
QH541.S647 2014
577.16—dc23
                                                                    2013026791

Manufactured in the United States of America.

Photo credits
Cover: Shutterstock: Manamana fg, Dmitry Naumov bg. Inside: Dreamstime: Andreus 7, Chanwangrong 5l, Costa007 22, F2 26, HongChan001 4b, Justinplunkett 15, Qnjt 18, Subie2 28, Winnond 6; Shutterstock: Almondd 25t, Aquapix 23br, Artcasta 5cl, Balounm 27t, Paul Banton 21cr, BHJ 8, Stephane Bidouze 23b, Aleksander Bolbot 17, Sylvie Bouchard 27r, Moritz Buchty 23tr, Hung Chung Chih 9, Ciurzynski 23tl, Claffra 5r, CreativeNature.nl 19c, Maksym Deliyergiyev 27b, Dennis Donohue 13, FormosanFish 5fr, Karel Gallas 14–15, Piotr Gatlik 21cl, Hecke61 25b, Iladm 25c, Sergey Krasnoshchokov 27r, LeonP 21tr, Richard Lister 20–21, Manamana 1fg, Xavier Marchant 23t, Jan Miko 5fl, Migel 29, Mlorenz 19t, Dmitry Naumov 1bg, Alta Oosthuizen 10–11, Plavevski 11, Andrey Pavlov 12, Tom Reichner 5cr, Ian Rentoul 4t, Leena Robinson 4c, Valery Shanin 19b, Graeme Shannon 21b, Smuay 16, Tntphototravis 24–25, Mogens Trolle 21tl, Joost van Uffelen 23bl.

CONTENTS

ALL ABOUT FOOD

Every living thing needs food to survive. Food gives living things the energy they need to live, grow, and move. When a rabbit eats grass, it gets energy from that food. When a fox eats a rabbit, it takes in energy stored in the rabbit's body. Energy flows from one living thing to another when it is eaten. This can be shown as a food chain.

Fox

Rabbit

Grass

> A food chain is named for the way the living things in it are linked together.

Snail

Minnow

Moose

Dipper

Water weed

Caddis fly larvae

In a food web, arrows show how energy flows between living things.

Sometimes, several different animals eat the same foods. On African grasslands, zebra, antelope, and wildebeest all eat grass, and they are all are eaten by lions and hyenas. Many food chains that are linked are called a food web.

THINK ABOUT IT
What did you eat for lunch today? Can you figure out your own food chain?

PRODUCERS

Plants do not eat food for energy. They make, or produce, their own food. That is why they are known as producers. Plants use water and a gas, called carbon dioxide, to make food in their leaves. This is called photosynthesis. Plants get energy for this process from sunlight. The sun is at the start of every food chain or web.

A plant's leaves are its food factories!

THINK ABOUT IT
Plants kept in the dark often die. Why does this happen?

To make food, plants take carbon dioxide from the air into their leaves. They take in water through their roots. A green substance in the leaves, called chlorophyll, traps energy from sunlight. The energy turns the gas and water into sugar and oxygen. The sugar is stored by the plant, to use as food. The oxygen goes back into the air.

Oxygen

Sunlight

Carbon dioxide

Water

Plant Eaters

You, your family, classmates, and every type of animal are consumers. Consumers are living things that consume, or eat, other living things to get energy. Animals that eat plants are called herbivores. Herbivores are the second link in a food chain or web. They take in the energy, produced by photosynthesis, that is stored in plant parts.

Sugar made by photosynthesis is found in different plant parts, from the plant's roots to its leaves.

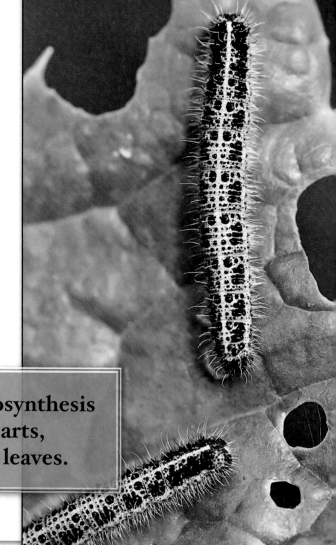

Herbivores eat whole plants, or certain parts of plants, to get the energy they need. Butterflies feed on the sweet nectar made in flowers. Mole rats burrow underground and eat plant roots. Giant pandas eat bamboo stems, and sparrows eat seeds.

THINK ABOUT IT
Sheep and horses' front teeth are oval or shovel shaped and their back teeth are square. How do these teeth help the animals get energy from grass?

Very large herbivores may have to eat huge amounts of plants to get enough energy.

Meat Eaters

Blue whales, crocodiles, and centipedes are all meat-eating consumers, or carnivores. Some carnivores eat herbivores. For example, tigers eat grass-eating deer and foxes eat rabbits. Some carnivores eat other carnivores, too. For example, killer whales eat sea lions, which eat fish. The bigger the carnivore, the more it has to eat.

COMPARE AND CONTRAST Scorpions, cobras, and jellyfish use venom to help them catch prey. Think about how they do this.

Lions eat most parts of the animals that they hunt and catch, from blood and muscle to skin and even bone.

Carnivores have many special features to help them catch their prey. These can include sharp teeth and good eyesight. Sea turtles have spikes in their mouth to catch slippery jellyfish. Spiders spin webs to catch flies. Humpback whales blow rings of bubbles to trap fish they then swallow.

Alligators hide in the water until prey moves close. Then the alligators pounce!

OMNIVORES

Do you eat meat, fruit, and vegetables? Then you are an omnivore. Omnivores are consumers that eat both plants and animals. That includes not only meat, but also other foods that animals produce, such as milk or eggs. Some omnivores have features for eating different foods. For example, raccoons have sharp front teeth for biting meat and flat back teeth for chewing plants.

Ants are omnivores that eat seeds, nectar, and insects.

THINK ABOUT IT Blackbirds eat worms and berries. What do you think other bird omnivores, such as ostriches and crows, eat?

Piranhas are fish that have razor-sharp teeth and are famous for killing other animals. However, they also eat underwater plants. Many animals eat both plants and meat to survive when the place where they live changes. For example, grizzly bears survive cold winters, when there are fewer animals to eat, by eating moss, seaweed, or berries.

Only around one-third of a grizzly bear's diet is meat, such as salmon. The rest is mostly plant parts.

SCAVENGERS

Scavengers mostly eat the bodies of dead animals and animal waste. Crabs, eels, vultures, and blowflies are all scavengers. Some carnivores scavenge when they cannot hunt. For example, lone hyenas eat the bones of dead animals, but packs of hyenas hunt together. Scavengers often have an excellent sense of smell to help them find rotting flesh to eat.

Vultures use their excellent eyesight to spot dead animals from high in the air.

Scavengers help to clear away the remains of dead animals. This is important because it helps decomposers to do their work.

It is easier for gulls to feed on food scraps at wasteyards than to hunt animals to eat.

Decomposers

Decomposers are the last links in food chains and food webs. They include fungi, such as mushrooms, and tiny living things called bacteria. Decomposers feed on the remains of living things, from dead leaves to pieces of food left over by scavengers. When maggots hatch from eggs on a dead animal, they spread bacteria over the body as they feed on it.

Maggots help decomposers by breaking up dead animals and waste into smaller pieces.

We see only part of fungi on the surface of the ground. The rest of a fungus is a big, hidden network underground that breaks down remains.

Decomposers, such as bacteria, break down waste and animal remains into nutrients. Nutrients are substances that all living things need to live. Rain washes nutrients into the soil. The nutrients help more plants to grow. By recycling nutrients, decomposers start new food chains and webs.

Recycling is changing waste so that it can be useful again.

FORESTS

In any forest, the main producers are trees. These plants have strong, thick trunks that hold up many branches and leaves. Animals consume many parts of trees. Deer eat bark, caterpillars eat leaves, and monkeys eat fruit. Consumers that hunt prey in forests include snakes, jaguars, and hawks.

COMPARE AND CONTRAST
The types of tree and consumer in warm forests are very different from those in forests that grow in cold places. Compare and contrast a food chain from each.

Some snakes move among branches to find food, such as bird eggs.

Dead leaves collect on the forest floor. Scavengers, such as woodlice and millipedes, eat this waste. Fungi decompose what is left. The nutrients they release help make rich soil in which tree seeds grow into new trees.

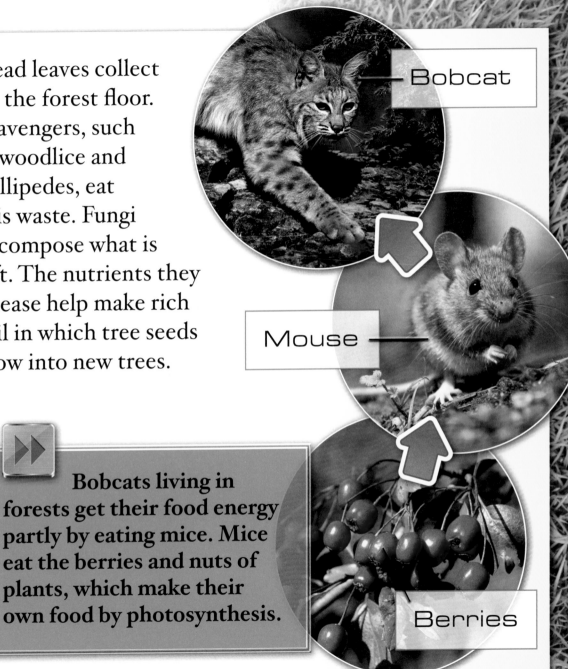

Bobcat

Mouse

Berries

Bobcats living in forests get their food energy partly by eating mice. Mice eat the berries and nuts of plants, which make their own food by photosynthesis.

Grasslands

The main types of plants that grow in grasslands are tough grasses. Grasslands are too dry for many trees to grow there. Grassland herbivores are adapted to get energy from grasses. For example, bison have several stomachs to digest, or break down, the grasses.

THINK ABOUT IT
Prairie dogs and rabbits are grassland herbivores. What do these animals do to keep out of sight of animals that might want to eat them?

▶▶ Zebras spend almost two-thirds of their time eating grass to get enough energy to survive.

Grassland carnivores include lions and cheetahs, which hunt zebra and antelope. They also include tiny ticks that climb from the grass onto animals to suck their blood. Grassland food webs also include scavengers, such as vultures and dung beetles, that feed on animal waste.

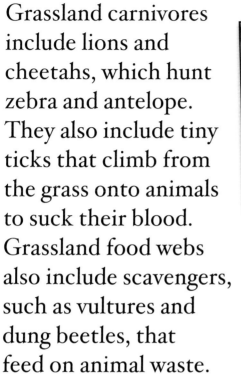

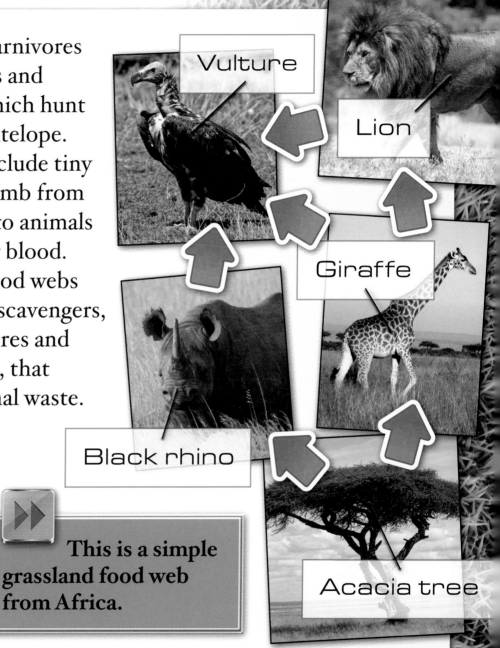

Vulture

Lion

Giraffe

Black rhino

Acacia tree

⏩ **This is a simple grassland food web from Africa.**

Oceans

Ocean food chains and webs begin with plantlike living things called algae. Like plants, algae make their food by photosynthesis. Seaweeds are algae. There are also billions of very tiny algae in the sea. Animals such as baby crabs and jellyfish eat the algae. These small animals are eaten by a wide range of fish, such as sardines.

Algae floats near the water's surface so it can get light for photosynthesis.

Ocean animals, including tuna, penguins, and dolphins, eat fish. These animals may become prey for sharks and whales. Dead ocean animals sink to the seafloor, where they are eaten by worms, starfish, and other scavengers.

Leopard seal

Killer Whale

Adélie penguin

Algae

Baleen whale

Krill

This is an example of an ocean food web.

COMPARE AND CONTRAST
Blue whales and whale sharks are the largest ocean animals. Compare and contrast how they feed by filtering animals from the water they swallow.

DESERTS

A desert is any large region that gets very little rain each year. In a desert near the equator, it is boiling hot by day and freezing cold at night. The biggest desert plants are cacti. Whenever it rains, cacti swell up to store water inside their tough stems. Their leaves are tough spikes, to help stop animals from eating them. Herbivores, such as finches, tortoises, gerbils, and camels, eat desert plant parts, from cactus flowers to grass seeds.

THINK ABOUT IT
A camel's hump is made of fat. It shrinks when the camel cannot find food. What causes this?

The cactus wren is a desert omnivore that sometimes eats nectar from cactus flowers.

Many desert herbivores are active at night, when it is coolest. Carnivores have different ways of finding prey in the dark. Rattlesnakes can sense the heat that prey, such as mice, make. Fennec foxes have giant ears to hear their prey moving.

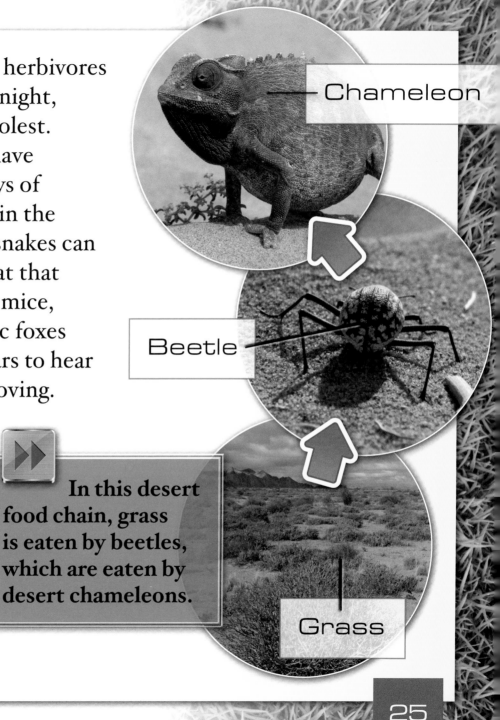

Chameleon

Beetle

Grass

In this desert food chain, grass is eaten by beetles, which are eaten by desert chameleons.

The Arctic

The Arctic is the freezing area around the North Pole. Algae grow under ice that floats in the Arctic Ocean. These algae are eaten by small ocean animals, such as shrimps. The shrimps are eaten by fish, such as arctic cod. Seals, seabirds, and whales eat fish and other animals, including crabs. Polar bears hunt seals when they come to the surface to breathe through holes in the floating ice.

▶▶ Seals hunt in water and return to land or ice to rest.

This is an Arctic food web on land. There are different food webs in the Arctic ocean.

Arctic wolf

Musk oxen

Caribou

Lichen

The only producers that survive on Arctic land include lichens and small shrubs. Caribou and enormous, shaggy musk oxen are the largest animals that eat these plants. They are hunted by packs of wolves.

THINK ABOUT IT
Many different seals also live in Antarctica, which is the region surrounding the South Pole. They include the leopard seal. What do you think this carnivore eats?

ALL CHANGE

When one type of animal is killed, it affects other links in the food chain or food web. People cause changes when they hunt animals, turn forests into farmland, or bring new animals to a place. For example, farmers brought cane toads to Australia to kill rats that ate their crops. Cane toads kill the animals that eat them, because they have poisonous skin.

▶▶ When people catch too many fish, they change the balance in ocean food chains and webs.

Some tigers can live safely in areas of protected land called preserves.

THINK ABOUT IT
Large sharks eat rays and rays eat scallops. Today, people hunt too many sharks. They use their fins to make soup. What is the effect of this on scallops?

We can help food chains and webs by protecting the places where plants and animals live. We can protect living things by making it against the law to hunt or harm them. How can you help food chains and webs?

GLOSSARY

adapted Having a special feature or way of behaving that helps a living thing to survive.

algae A plantlike living thing that can make its own food by photosynthesis.

bacteria Tiny living things that can help us, but that can also cause diseases.

carbon dioxide A colorless, odorless gas found in the air.

carnivores Animals that eat other animals.

consumers Living things that get food and energy by eating (consuming) other living things.

decomposers The fungi and bacteria that feed on the remains of living things left behind by scavengers.

energy Power that can make things work, move, live, and grow.

equator An imaginary circle around the Earth equally distant from the North pPole and the South Pole.

filtering Sifting something, such as water, to remove objects from it.

fungi Living things that grow on plants or rotting matter. (Fungi is the plural form of fungus.)

gas A substance, such as air, that we cannot usually see.

grasslands Areas of land covered mainly in grasses.

herbivores Animals that eat only plants.

krill Small shrimplike creatures found in oceans.

maggots Wormlike baby flies that feed on rotting animals, plants, and waste.

nectar The sugary juice found in the middle of a flower.

nutrients Substances that living things need to live.

omnivores Animals that eat plants and other animals.

oxygen A gas in the air around us.

prey Animals hunted for food.

producers Living things that produce or make their own food.

roots The parts of a plant that grow into the soil.

seeds The parts of a plant made by flowers that can grow into a new plant.

stems The parts of plants that hold up a leaves and flowers.

venom Poison made by animals.

waste Urine or feces.

FOR MORE INFORMATION

Books

Amstutz, Lisa J. and Anne Wertheim. *What Eats What in a Rain Forest Food Chain* (Food Chains). North Mankato, MN: Picture Window Books, 2012.

Fronczak, Emerson. *There's a Food Chain in Your Garden!* (Infomax Common Core Readers). New York, NY: Rosen Classroom, 2013.

Gray, Leon. *Food Webs* (Life Science Stories). New York, NY: Gareth Stevens Publishing, 2013.

Hawley, Ella. *Exploring Food Chains and Food Webs* (Let's Explore Life Science). New York, NY: Powerkids Press, 2012.

Solway, Andrew. *Food Chains and Webs* (Raintree Freestyle Express: The Web of Life). North Mankato, MN: Heinemann-Raintree, 2012.

Websites

Due to the changing nature of Internet links, Rosen Publishing has developed an online list of Websites related to the subject of this book. This site is updated regularly. Please use this link to access the list:

http://www.rosenlinks.com/lfo/food

INDEX